The Letters of
SAINT PATRICK

JOHN LUCE and MARCUS LOSACK

Published in Ireland by

CÉILE DÉ
Castlekevin
Annamoe
Co Wicklow

The following translation of Saint Patrick's Confession and Letter to Coroticus is by John Luce (2009) revised by Marcus Losack, based on the Latin texts published by L. Bieler in Libri Epistolarum Sancti Patricii Episcopi, R.I.A., Dublin, 1993, and D. R. Howlett, The Book of Letters of Saint Patrick the Bishop, Dublin 1994. Chapter numbers given follow Bieler's numerical divisions.

First Edition
St Patrick's Day, 2015.

ISBN 978-1-909751-30-9

THIS BOOK IS DEDICATED TO

JOHN VICTOR LUCE
(1921–2011)

ILLUSTRATIONS

Front Cover: Image of St Patrick in stained glass from Down Cathedral, Downpatrick, Co Down.

Inside front cover: St Patrick baptizing Irish princesses. From John H. Haaren and A.B. Poland, *Famous Men of the Middle Ages*, © Renaissance Classics, USA, 1904.

The Saint Patrick of Ancient Ages, page 8.

An extract of Fol. 23 from St Patrick's Confession (C:14) from Gwynn's Facsimile of the Book of Armagh, 1837, page 26.

An extract of Fol. 21 from St Patrick's Confession (C:1) from Gwynn's Facsimile of the Book of Armagh, 1937, page 28.

Patrick and three relics of Book, Bell and Staff. Saint Patrick's Cathedral (Cof I) Armagh, page 32.

Image of St Patrick as a slave, Down Cathedral, page 34.

Image of Saint Patrick from Magheralin Parish Church Craigavon, Co. Down, page 64.

Interior stairs at Dumbarton Castle: Pernot, 1827, page 72.

Inside back cover: A map by Réne Henry showing the ancient forest of Quokelunde, old Gallic-Roman roads and the coastline between Aleth (St Malo) and Mont St Michel at the time of St Patrick, before an inundation of the sea © Éditions La Découvrance, La Rochelle, 2006.

Photographs on the front cover and on pages 32, 34 and 64 are by Gigliola Siragusa © Gigliola Siragusa, 2014.

CONTENTS

The Saint Patrick of Ancient Ages.

The Letters of
SAINT PATRICK

PREFACE

This is a radical, new translation of the two letters
written by St Patrick that have survived in
various manuscript copies since the fifth century. For
the first time in the long history of Patrician Studies,
the Latin phrase 'in Britanniis', which is the name
given for St Patrick's homeland as it appears in the
earliest surviving copy of Patrick's Confession,
preserved in the Book of Armagh, is translated as 'in
Brittany' rather than 'in Britain'.

This is based on consideration of all the evidence
available in the primary and secondary sources and
acceptance of the fact that Brittany was known as
Britanniis or *Britannia* at the time of St Patrick's birth
(c. 385 CE) as a result of a strategic settlement of the
ancient Britons in Armorica during the rebellion of
Magnus Maximus, who ruled as Emperor of the West
from 385-389 CE. If Patrick was born in Brittany in
385 CE or moved there as an infant with his family
as part of this migration, then he would have grown
up understanding 'Britanniis' to be his homeland.

Several of the early 'Lives' of St Patrick published
by Fr John Colgan in 1647 in his book *Trias*

Thaumaturga, record that Patrick was taken captive from a region called 'Armoric Letha' or 'Lethania Britannia'. Both these places can be identified with Armorica (Brittany) and the ancient Roman port at Aleth (St Malo) where the Legion of Mars was stationed at the close of the fourth century.

Most scholars today hold fast to the traditional theory that St Patrick came from Britain and was taken captive from Britain. The notion that he was taken captive from Brittany, however, is a view shared by the majority of early Breton historians and several other Irish and continental writers, ancient and modern. The arguments in favour can be found in the recently published books *Rediscovering Saint Patrick – A New Theory of Origins* (Marcus Losack, Columba Press, Dublin, 2013) and *St Patrick and the Bloodline of the Grail – the Untold Story of St Patrick's Royal Family* (Céile Dé, Castlekevin, Annamoe, Co. Wicklow, 2013). In the author's opinion, all five of the key geographical references related to his place of origins which appear in St Patrick's Confession can now be identified in Brittany.

This includes Patrick's homeland 'in Britanniis' (C:23,32,43) which can be located within Brittany and not the island of Britain, exclusively. Secondly, the villa and estate near 'Bannavem Tiburniae' from which Patrick was taken captive, may be identified with the site where Château de Bonaban is now located, on the northeast coast of Brittany, in the village of La Gouesnière, between the old Roman port at Aleth (St

Malo) and Dol de Bretagne. This small, French country château is built on a very ancient and strategic site where Celtic axes and remains of a bathhouse or swimming pool from the late Roman period have been discovered, as recorded by Joseph Viel in his book *La Gouesnière et Bonaban* (1913).

The place from which St Patrick was taken captive has never been securely identified. Strathclyde in Scotland, Cumbria, Wales, the Severn Valley and even Glastonbury in England have been suggested by various scholars. Most of the early Breton historians insist that it was located within a very specific local geographical region on the northeast coast of Brittany, in the cantons of Letha between Aleth (St Malo), Dol de Bretagne and Mont St Michel.

This would accord with the fifth 'Life of St Patrick' by Probus, published by Fr. Colgan, which states that Patrick was taken captive from Brittany. M. Charles de Gerville, a Breton antiquarian writing in the 1840s, is credited with being the first to claim that the estate owned by Calpurnius, existed on or close to the site where Château de Bonaban is now located.

An archaeological excavation would be the surest way to clarify this important historical issue. Should this confirm the existence of a private villa during the late Roman period, it would provide further evidence to support the case that it could be the place where St Patrick once lived before he was taken captive by Irish pirates and sold as a slave in Ireland.

Thirdly, the Wood of Foclud, which Patrick remembered in the context of a dream or nightmare that he experienced after escaping from slavery in Ireland (C:23) may be identified with the ancient forest of Quokelunde which existed in the lowland, coastal area surrounding the present site of the Château before it was submerged by an inundation of the sea. A local tradition recorded in Brittany describes how Irish pirates landed nearby at Cancale and crept up through this forest before they attacked the estate owned by Calpurnius and took St Patrick captive.

Fourthly, the Latin 'Mare Occidentale', which St Patrick also mentioned in the context of that dream when he described the Wood of Foclud as being 'close beside the Western Sea' (C:23), can be identified with the ocean that extends westwards from the coast of Brittany and not the Atlantic Ocean off the west coast of Ireland, as has traditionally been assumed.

Finally, when St Patrick says he longed to leave Ireland and return to visit his homeland 'in Britanniis' to see members of his surviving or extended family and then proceed further 'into the Gauls' (Galliis) to visit some of his religious brethren and 'see the faces of the saints of my Lord' for whom he held great affection, this longing in his heart can be understood firstly as a reference to Brittany and then to the community of St Martin at Tours with which Patrick was associated, having spent time there during his religious training (C:43). St Martin's monastery was located on the other side of the River Loire and within 'the Galls'. The coastal region of Brittany that Patrick knew as his homeland was distinguished from Roman Gaul in local ethnic geography at the end of the fourth century, as a result of civil wars and rebellions that affected the whole region at that time. 'Britanniis' (La Petite Bretagne or Britannia Minor) was thus eventually distinguished from the island of greater Britain and replaced Armorica as the name for this coastal region we now call Brittany.

The origins of 'proto-Bretagne' and the precise date when this region became known as 'Britannia' or 'Britanniis' is historically controversial but there is evidence to suggest this name change took place at the time of the rebellion of Maximus in 383 CE, if not significantly before.

PATRICK'S RELIGIOUS TRAINING

St. Patrick's connections with Brittany go far deeper than many Patrician scholars have been willing or able to accept. Other references to Brittany mentioned by the majority of early Breton historians and preserved in the ancient, secondary sources deserve to be given greater attention. The ancient Life of St Patrick written by Probus claims that Patrick was instructed for four years within St Martin's community before he undertook several years of further training and spiritual formation with a group of 'barefoot hermits' in the 'Isles of the Tyrrhene Sea'. The location of these islands, in relation to traditions associated with St Patrick, has never been clearly established but this may be a reference to islands or early monastic communities that once existed off the north east coast of Brittany. Modern geography locates the Tyrrhene Sea in the Mediterranean north of Sicily but this was not always the case. It can also be identified with the Bay of Mont St Michel, not far from Château de Bonaban.

A local tradition preserved in Brittany, in accord with the Life of Patrick by Probus, claims that St Patrick was ordained and commissioned for his Mission to Ireland by a bishop called 'Saint Senior'. He is remembered as one of the founding apostles of Neustria and was associated with Mont St Michel, today a famous place of pilgrimage and a UNESCO World Heritage site. A local parish church dedicated to St Senior exists today at nearby Avranches and there are other sites and churches associated with St Patrick in this region.

This includes the ancient parish of St Patrice-du-Teilleul and a locality called Bourg de Saint Patrice with a small chapel dedicated to St Patrick, dating to the sixth or seventh century. At Saint Patrice-de-Claids, near Coutances, the ruins of another church dedicated to Patrick survive with an early statue of him carrying a cross, preserved in an alcove. An old Roman road passed through the territory of Saint Patrice, which indicates the antiquity of the site. The association between St Patrick and various places in Brittany is very significant.

At St Servan, which is now a suburb of St Malo where the Roman port at Alet once dominated the mouth of the River Rance, the foundations of an ancient church are preserved together with Roman remains from occupation as early as the first century. It is possible that St Patrick's father, as a Decurion, may have been familiar with this site. It was a provincial centre for Roman military and political administration and provided a residence for the Prefect of the Legion of Mars (*Legio Martenensis*), stationed there in the closing decades of the fourth century. There is a beautiful Catholic church dedicated to St Patrick in this modern suburb of St Malo and the old road that links the village of La Gouesnière and Château de Bonaban with St Servan is still called La rue d'Alet, reminding us of its ancient and historical significance.

THE STAFF OF JESUS

One of several intriguing legends surrounding St Patrick states that he was given a religious staff (akin to a crosier) by a hermit living on one of the mysterious 'Isles of the Tyrrhene Sea' close to Mont St Michel (possibly Tombelaine).

This sacred staff was said to have once been carried by Jesus Christ and that it was preserved for St Patrick because he was called to be the 'Last of the Apostles' through whom the Lord's commandment was to be fulfilled, that the Gospel should be preached 'to the ends of the Earth' – at that time a reference to Ireland as the Americas had yet to be discovered.

The famous staff was known in Ireland as the 'Baccail Isu' or Staff of Jesus, and was long treasured by the Irish Church as the most important relic of Saint Patrick until it was lost (possibly destroyed) in Dublin at the time of the Reformation. St Bernard of Clairvaux, writing in the twelfth century, refers to St Patrick's Staff as conferring more power than the highest canonical sanction. He describes it as being overlaid with gold, adorned with the most precious jewels and treasured in Ireland as one of the relics of St Patrick given the highest dignity and veneration.

SAINT PATRICK'S ROYAL FAMILY

Other intriguing statements recorded by several early Breton historians and found in various genealogical tables, suggest that St Patrick came from a noble family of the ancient Britons, linked to the ancient Kings of Dalriada whose stronghold was at Dumbarton, in what is now Scotland. At the time of St Patrick the River Clyde separated the Britons in the south from the Scots (Irish) of Dalriada to the north. The Gaelic kingdom of Dalriada existed on both sides of the Irish Sea, including Co. Antrim in the north of Ireland together with Argyll and the Western Highlands and Islands in Scotland, as far south as the River Clyde.

The Kingdom of Strathclyde extended from the River Derwent in Cumberland to the Firth of Clyde; its population came from two British peoples (as opposed to Anglo-Saxons, Picts or Scots-Irish). The Cymric or Welsh were in the south while the northern part was occupied by the Damnonii who were Cornish. The capital of this ancient kingdom was the heavily fortified rock on the Clyde, called by the Britons 'Alcluid', now known as Dumbarton (Dun Briton) – the Fort of the Britons. This is said to be one of the oldest castles in Britain.

Saint Patrick's second letter was written to Coroticus, a British king and warlord in control of the Kingdom of Strathclyde from about 450-470 CE. He was the founder of a famous dynasty that ruled Strathclyde down to the eighth century. Patrick's family is closely associated with Strathclyde in some of the ancient sources. The claim that he was born on the banks of the Clyde still forms part of the Scottish historical record. Breton historians record that Calpurnius was a 'Scottish' prince who migrated with his family to Brittany at the time of the rebellion of Maximus in 383 CE. There were also strong family ties with Gaul. Patrick's mother, Concessa, was 'of the Franks' and a niece of St Martin of Tours.

In these accounts, St Patrick belonged to a royal family linked to the ancient Kings of Scotland and the House of Wales and Brittany, from which the early Breton aristocracy is descended. This includes the historically elusive Conan, said to have been appointed the first king in Brittany as a result of the support he gave to Maximus during the rebellion.

After the death of his first wife Ursula, in tragic circumstances, Conan married Patrick's sister, Darerca. Another sister of St Patrick called Tigris, married Grallon who was crowned the second king of Brittany after the death of his father, Conan. These events are said to have taken place in the period 383-425 CE. A third sister of St Patrick called Cinnemon, is remembered in Ireland as 'Royal Cinne'.

Then there is St Patrick himself. In his Letter to Coroticus, Patrick states clearly that he 'sold his nobility' for the sake of others. The Latin phrase given is 'vendidi enim nobilitatem meam', which can be translated 'I sold my royal entitlement for the sake of others' (LC:10). St Patrick may have done this for religious reasons or to help finance his Mission to Ireland. His sisters would never have held such high aristocratic status without the existence of a proven pedigree.

Genealogical tables (especially the ancient ones) and later hagiographical and ecclesiastical traditions cannot be taken as reliable historical evidence, but if there is any truth in the claim that St Patrick came from a noble family of the ancient Britons who formed part of the early Breton aristocracy at the time of the Emperor Magnus Maximus in 383 CE, this not only strengthens the case for locating St Patrick's homeland in Brittany, it surely confirms it.

St Patrick's understanding of Christianity may have been influenced by his family and ancestral heritage as well as religious and spiritual formation in Brittany, where a vibrant Jewish-Christian community existed with a strong allegiance to Judaic as well as Messianic traditions. The fourth *Life of St Patrick* published by John Colgan in 1647 begins with an intriguing statement:

> The Elders declare that St Patrick was of Jewish origin. After our Lord had died on the cross for the sins of the human race, the Roman army, avenging his Passion, laid waste Judea, and Jews taken captive were dispersed amongst all the nations of the earth. Some settled among the Armoric Britons (in Brittany) and it is stated that it was from them Patrick traced his origins.

In a *Life of Patrick* from the Book of Lismore, this dispersion of St Patrick's ancestors from the Holy Land to Brittany is said to have taken place following the destruction of the Temple in Jerusalem and devastation in Judea by Titus and Vespasian in 70 CE.

THE LAST APOSTLE

St Patrick was an outstandingly courageous and deeply spiritual person, a man of great faith, commitment and resilience, one of the few Christian witnesses we have from the fifth century. We can certainly think of him as being 'The Last of the Apostles'. The command of Jesus to his disciples to carry the Gospel to the Ends of the Earth was fulfilled in Patrick's Mission to Ireland. St Patrick stands at the very portal of Irish history, at the beginning of the Dark Ages in Europe that followed the collapse of the Roman Empire, before the Golden Age of Celtic Christianity (500-1000 CE). Despite many centuries of historical uncertainty and having grown up with the traditional view that St Patrick came from Britain and was taken captive from Britain, hopefully we can now begin to know something of the truth by understanding the historical context that provides a foundation for his biography.

This includes, for example, the places that he may have remembered from his childhood in Brittany, the location for those traumatic events that took place on the day when he was taken captive by Irish pirates. These are the events that shaped St Patrick's life and destiny.

Saint Patrick's Letters are authentic, historical documents that can be dated from internal evidence to the fifth century. They testify to his understanding of the demands of faith and the practice of Christianity. His strong faith, courage and spiritual integrity provides a portal through which we can understand, appreciate and know him, as well as our own historical and religious identity, our cultural heritage and the importance of his legacy.

For St Patrick, Christianity had not lost its material and spiritual obligations or its call to adventure and creative social and religious reform, as so often appears to be the case today. His Letters offer a remarkable insight into social, political and religious ethics and the strong beliefs of a person who gave his whole life to God. The call to follow Christ required renunciation of wealth and status, voluntary exile from homeland and family and a total disclosure of the heart before God – an arena in which so many saints were fashioned.

How and where St Patrick died we shall probably never know. From the way he chose to end his Confession, he clearly sensed that his own death was immanent. St Patrick's Letter to Coroticus is an angry, grief-filled and very challenging letter; it threatens the king with damnation if he does not make recompense for acts of violence and abuse perpetrated against Patrick's recent converts in Ireland. The missive (which Patrick wanted to make public) must have been received by the king as extremely threatening and provocative, despite the olive branch of promised forgiveness and reconciliation offered at the end. In the context of these events, it is possible that St Patrick suffered a martyr's death, perhaps as a direct consequence of writing this letter and his obvious determination to secure the return of female converts who had been abducted.

Now Patrick had to come to terms with death and what happens on the borderline between this world and the next.

Death was for him nothing to be feared, nor was it the end of his adventure in faith but simply to be embraced as the next stage in a more mysterious journey, through which all he came to believe in during his life and longed for in his heart could now be fulfilled.

Patrick's theology relies heavily on teachings from the Hebrew Scriptures with several quotations and biblical references to Mosaic Law and the Prophets. There is a strong eschatological and almost 'Messianic' twist to his understanding of history. The Gospel had been preached in Ireland and this marked the beginning of the End of Time. In his Confession, St Patrick gives thanks to God that 'we have all seen it happen now, so it is accomplished; the Gospel has been proclaimed in those places beyond which there is no human habitation' (C:34). He believed that since this biblical obligation had now been fulfilled, through his mission to Ireland, 'the end would come' (C:40). There is a deeply personal and almost lyrical and structured, poetic style to Saint Patrick's way of communicating that gives his words the impact of an inspiring religious storyteller and powerful teacher and preacher who speaks with such conviction it can stir the pilgrim heart and soul in every generation.

Apart from St Patrick's Letters, no reliable historical information about him has survived from the fifth century. We must give thanks to Patrick for sharing his story with us and also to the scribes and scholars who made copies of the manuscripts down through the centuries, for without them we would have been left completely in the dark.

There is so much about St Patrick and his family that remains a mystery but we can more fully appreciate his writings, when we consider that it is nothing short of a miracle that these letters have survived through the darkest turmoil of history and the changing fortunes of time.

NOTES ON THIS TRANSLATION

The following translation of St Patrick's Confession and Letter to Coroticus is by John Luce (2009) former Professor of Classics and Public Orator at Trinity College Dublin, adapted and revised by Marcus Losack (2010). Elements from previous editions published by N.J. White (1905) Ludwig Bieler (1962) Daniel Conneely (1979) David Howlett (1994) and Padraig McCarthy (2003) as well as others are included where considered appropriate.

The earliest surviving copy of St Patrick's Confession is preserved in the Book of Armagh, Trinity College, Dublin (TCD MS52) written by the scribe Ferdomhnach in 807 CE.

For copies of this and other manuscripts with translation in various languages and an extensive bibliography, see the Royal Irish Academy's website www.confessio.ie. Online resources that have been helpful include CELT, University College, Cork, Corpus of Electronic Texts, www.celt.ucc.ie and

Project Gutenberg, *The Most Ancient Lives of Saint Patrick*, www.gutenberg.org. Google Books has provided an excellent resource for students through the digitalization programme, including many of the works of the early Breton historians.

Certain decisions with regard to translation require explanation. At the beginning of Patrick's Confession the Latin name 'decurione', which describes the status of Calpurnius, has been included because of St Patrick's statement in his Letter to Coroticus, 'decurione patre nascor', meaning 'I am the son of a Decurion' (LC:10). The word deacon in the Book of Armagh appears to be an interpolation, reflecting later ecclesiastical influences. Likewise, the Greek word 'Helia' which refers to the Sun (C:20), has sometimes been transcribed as 'Helias' and translated as meaning Elias or Elijah. In his experience of excruciating pain when he was attacked, St Patrick appears in desperation to have invoked the Sun, although it is possible that his words were chosen because of their biblical association with Jesus' experience on the Cross, where it was thought that he was calling Elijah (Matthew 27:46,47).

In some of the most accredited translations of St Patrick's Confession, Patrick's homeland 'in Britanniis' (C:23, 32, 43) is rendered as Britain, reflecting the established and widely accepted theory of origins and referring to the island of Britain exclusively. Other scholars have been more cautious, translating this as 'in the Britains' which retains the uncertainty characteristic of the original Latin phrase found in the Book of Armagh, where it consistently appears in a plural form. When Professor Luce kindly translated St Patrick's Letters for me, he suggested that 'in Britanniis' should best be translated as 'in the Britains' or 'among the Britons' but agreed with a proposal that if this was possibly a reference to the region we now call Brittany then it would be legitimate to offer a revised English translation using the singular form 'in Brittany', to provide greater historical and geographical clarity for the modern reader.

When he sent me his final text, I was surprised and delighted to see that he had actually included Brittany as his preferred translation. I am and will forever be indebted to Professor Luce for freely giving of his time and talents to complete a translation of St Patrick's Letters for me. John was an expert Latinist and when I asked for his assistance, he embraced this opportunity in the final years of his retirement with great enthusiasm. He provided a scholarly translation in English that he believed was in keeping with the original Latin texts and this was revised slightly to reflect the personal nature of Patrick's style of writing in a way that hopefully catches something of the spirit of St Patrick's literary and ecclesiastical genius.

There is an intriguing sentence in St Patrick's Confession (C:14) that almost defies translation, including a word (or phrase) that may have been misunderstood or misrepresented. The word "ex/agallias" appears in the Book of Armagh, divided between the end of one line and the beginning of another. The scribe has written a note in the margin saying, "incertus liber" which means 'the book is uncertain'. This informs the reader that the manuscript being copied, which may have been the original letter written by St Patrick, either could not be understood at this point, perhaps because it was damaged and not fully legible, or because the word or sentence in question had somehow caused confusion.

In other manuscripts of St Patrick's Confession that have survived, the word "exgallias" appears as one single word and it has also been recorded as "Gallicis". There has been some debate as to the correct spelling and precise meaning of these words in the context of St Patrick's letter.

Extract of Folio 23 from Gwynn's Facsimile of the Book of Armagh (1937) showing the controversial word or phrase "ex-agallias" with the scribe's marginal note, 'incertus liber'.

Sir Samuel Ferguson, who was addressing the Royal Irish Academy in Dublin (as President) in 1879, notes that it may refer to St Patrick's brothers and sons in

Gaul, or from Gaul. He also suggested that if this was a reference to Gaul, it would lend support to a Gallic theory of origins. In his view, however, the original in all three cases came from a single word "exagellae" that signifies a legacy, inheritance or bequest (following Du Cange). In translation, he chose to delete any reference to Gaul. Ludwig Bieler accepts that the meaning is obscure, but also takes the view (following Du Cange and Ferguson) that Patrick is referring to a legacy which he is bequeathing to his "brothers and sons". As a result, the possible reference to Gaul is again omitted and consequently lost in translation.

I did not have the opportunity to discuss this matter with Professor Luce, but colleagues in Italy who are Latinists have all taken the view that it is without doubt a reference to Gaul.

Even though the scribe in Armagh noted the obscurity, the most obvious interpretation from reading the texts is that Patrick was referring to Gaul or his Gallic "brothers" and the thousands of converts in Ireland that were baptised as a result of his (Patrick's) leaving Gaul. If so, these words have an intended meaning and context that goes beyond a general reference to what St Patrick is bequeathing as an inheritance for others. I have taken the view (following Betham) that "ex-agallias", "exgallias" and "Gallicis" are direct references to Gaul and the phrase "my Gallic brothers and my sons" has therefore now been included in translation.

Extract of Folio 21 of Saint Patrick's Confession (C:1) from Gwynn's facsimile of the Book of Armagh, 1937. 'Ego Patricius, peccator, rusticissimus' – My name is Patrick, the sinner without a formal education.

The precise meaning of the whole paragraph is still very uncertain. Does the "my brothers from Gaul" refer to St Patrick's religious colleagues, perhaps those he longed to see again who may have belonged to Martin's community at Tours, those from Gaul who participated in his Mission to Ireland and were resident in Ireland, or Gallic slaves who had been taken captive to Ireland? Likewise, do the "sons" of St Patrick refer to his Gallic sons or Irish sons, including or excluding those thousands he baptised in the Lord?

The reference to the thousands of converts that St Patrick had baptised suggests a possible association with the "thousands" he said were taken captive with him (C:1).If so, St Patrick's Mission may have focused on caring for those from his own country who were held captive in Ireland, as he once was, as well as proclaiming the Gospel to the native Irish (and others) amongst whom he resided. I must give thanks to Dr Gigliola Siragusa for drawing attention to the phrase "ex-agallias" and for her help as a consultant during the final edit of this book, pouring over the meaning of words in St Patrick's Confession with the aid of Latin Dictionaries and other linguistic resources in Italian, French and English.

We have learned from experience that it is impossible to write or publish anything about St Patrick without being controversial. Perhaps this is because conflict and controversy are ingrained within the very fabric of Patrick's life and legacy and his experience of God's calling (see "exagalliae" in D.R. Howlett, *The Book of Letters of Saint Patrick the Bishop*, Four Courts Press, Dublin, 1994, p. 121). The true nature and extent of St Patrick's associations with Gaul have always been controversial. A 'pro-British' and 'contra-Gallic' interpretation of the evidence has a very ancient and well established pedigree. It originated with Muirchú in the Book of Armagh and was present in the writings of Ussher, Colgan and the Bollandists, followed by many others. These scholars all had privileged access to the ancient manuscripts concerning St Patrick and their obvious prejudice in favour of Britain and against the evidence for Gaul reveals a partisan and political stance that has woven a powerful spell around our understanding of St Patrick even to the present day.

Patrician scholars in more recent times, have regurgitated the traditional British theory of origins as if it was infallible. This has been done without the presentation of a shred of tangible or even mildly convincing evidence. Perhaps the time has come for someone with the necessary academic expertise and authority, to break the "spell" of Britain once and for all? I am not writing as an academic historian, but simply, as someone with a passionate interest in Patrick's story, intrigued by the contradictions and uncertainties that surround his biography and fuelled by a life-long interest in the origins of Irish Christianity and the treasures of the Celtic Tradition. Scholars must continue to wrestle with the complex issues that have influenced our image and understanding of St Patrick but should not be afraid to question the historical integrity of established traditions.

Some will disagree and strongly challenge the fact that 'Britanniis' has been translated as Brittany rather than Britain. Professor Luce was supportive of this decision but his expertise was requested to provide a scholarly and literal translation. Any errors that may have occurred due to revisions of his text for the general reader and in light of my own personal belief that St Patrick was taken captive from Brittany are therefore entirely my responsibility.

We hope you can enjoy reading St Patrick's Letters now in the spirit with which they were written and in the context of a new translation and revised theory of origins in which Brittany plays such an important part.

Marcus Losack
IRELAND
Saint Patrick's Day, 2015.

Saint Patrick with three relics of Book, Bell and Staff, from a stained glass window in Saint Patrick's Cathedral, Armagh (CofI).
Photo by Gigliola Siragusa.

SAINT PATRICK'S CONFESSION

Image of Saint Patrick as a slave in Ireland. Down Cathedral.
Photo by Gigliola Siragusa.

ST PATRICK'S CONFESSION

1. MY NAME IS PATRICK, a sinner without education, least of all the faithful and greatly despised in the eyes of many. My father was Calpurnius, a Decurion, the son of Potitus, an elder in the village of *Bannavem Tiburniae*; he had a small estate nearby from where I was taken captive. I was about sixteen years of age at that time and ignorant of the one true God and I was taken captive to Ireland with thousands of people as we deserved because we had turned away from God and not kept the commandments; we were not obedient to our priests who used to admonish us about our salvation.

God brought upon us the anger of his Spirit and scattered us among many nations, even to the ends of the earth where now my insignificance is placed among strangers.

2. And there the Lord revealed to me the nature of my unbelief, so that even though it was late, I should recall my transgressions and turn with my whole heart to the Lord my God, who fixed his eyes on the desperate situation I was in and showed pity towards my young age and foolishness and kept guard over me even before I knew Him and before I could learn wisdom or distinguish between good and evil, and has protected me and consoled me as a father would his son.

3. That's why I cannot keep silent – and nor indeed should I – about the great benefits and grace which the Lord considered appropriate to bestow upon me in the land of my captivity because this is my service to be rendered in return, after being seized by an awareness of God's presence, to exalt and testify to his wonders in the presence of every nation under Heaven.

4. Because there is no other God, nor ever has been or will be except God the Father uncreated without beginning, from whom

comes all new beginnings, holding the whole universe as we have learned; and His Son, Jesus Christ, whom we testify to have been always with the Father, before the beginning of creation with the Father in spiritual fashion and in an unspeakable way manifest before all things.

And through Him all things were made visible and invisible. He was made man and having overcome death, was received into heaven by the Father and He gave Him all power over every name in heaven, on earth and under the earth, that every tongue should confess to Him that Jesus Christ is Lord and God. We believe in Him and expect his coming to take place soon as judge of the living and the dead, who shall render to each and all according to their deeds. He has poured out upon us in abundance the Holy Spirit, the gift and pledge of immortality, who makes those who are believers and obey the law to become the children of god and co-heirs with Christ, whom we confess and adore as one God in the Trinity of sacred Name.

5. For he has spoken through the prophet:
    'Call upon me in the time of trouble and I
    will help you, and you will glorify me'. And
    again he says: 'It is honorable to confess
    and manifest the works of God'.

6. Although I am imperfect in so many ways,
    I wish my religious community and
    extended family to know what sort of
    person I really am, so that they might
    understand the desire of my soul.

7. I am not ignorant of the testimony of my
    Lord, who bears witness in the psalm: 'You
    will destroy those who speak lies'. Again
    He says: 'The mouth that lies destroys the
    soul'. And the Lord says the same in the
    Gospel: 'The empty word spoken by
    human beings will have to be accounted for
    in the Day of Judgment'.

8. So, with fear and trembling, I should dread
    more than anything else that day when
    none shall be able to escape or hide but
    all – without exception – will have to
    give an account of even the smallest of

transgressions before the tribunal of Jesus Christ.

9. I have thought of writing about this for a long time but hesitated until now because I was afraid to enter the arena of speaking in public. I have not learned as well as others, those deeply immersed in both law and scripture, whose education since childhood was never interrupted but made more perfect. For my words and speech had to be translated into a language that was foreign to me; this is obvious from my writings, which reflect the way I have learned and been instructed in the art of using words, as scripture says: 'The wisdom of a person is revealed through the tongue, in respect of understanding and knowledge and ability to teach the truth'.

10. What use is there in making excuses, however legitimate they may be, especially considering how much now I seek to acquire in my old age that which I failed to achieve in my youth? The fact is that my sins impeded me from taking a firm grip

on what I had discerned before. But who believes me now, even though I am repeating what I said earlier?

As a teenager, in reality just a beardless boy, I learned about captivity, before I knew what to seek or what to avoid. That is why I am embarrassed and afraid of exposing my lack of education for I am unable to explain my self succinctly to those who are well educated; at least not in the way my soul and spirit long to do, to reflect my deeper feelings and mental disposition.

11. But even if the same gifts had been given to me as they have to others, I would not keep silent for fear of retribution. And if by chance some people think I am pushing myself forward too much because of my lack of knowledge and hesitant speech, nevertheless it is written: 'Even tongues that stammer shall quickly learn how to speak words of peace'. How much more should we strive to share this wisdom with others, those of us who are like a letter sent from Christ for the salvation of the whole

world, not necessarily eloquent but one engraved powerfully into your hearts, not with ink, but with the spirit of the living God. The Spirit bears witness again that even what comes from the countryside has been created by the Most High.

12. Because of my rural upbringing, I was basically an ignorant exile, unable to see what the future could hold, but one thing I know for certain, is that before my humiliation, I was like a stone lying deep in mire; and the Mighty One came and in his mercy sustained me and raised me up and placed me high on top of a wall, which is why I have a strong obligation to speak out loudly and give something back to the Lord for all His mercies and great benefits that he has given, both here and in eternity, which the human mind cannot fathom.

13. So be astonished and dumfounded, all you great and small who fear the Lord, and you haughty men of letters. Listen and consider this. Who was it that raised up a fool like me, above the ranks of those who are wise

and skilful in law, powerful in speech and successful in every accomplishment, in the eyes of men? And inspired me, the outcast of this world, ahead of all others, so that with reverence and respect and without complaint I should be a faithful servant to the people given to me in my lifetime by the love of Christ, should I prove worthy to be their humble, diligent and truthful, servant.

14. And so, in definition of faith in the Trinity, without shrinking from danger, it is necessary to emphasize and make known the gift of God and the consolations of eternity, with confidence and without wavering; to spread the name of God in every place, so that even after my death I can leave behind to my Gallic brothers and my sons, so many thousands of human beings whom I have baptized in the Lord.

15. I was not worthy or deserving that the Lord should concede this to me his servant, after such tribulations and difficulties in captivity; after so many years, that He would grant me such benevolence

with that people. It was something in my youth I could never have hoped for or imagined.

16. But after I came to Ireland, every day I had to tend cattle and many times I prayed throughout the day. The love of God surrounded me more and more and my faith and reverence towards God was strengthened and my spirit was moved so much that in a single day I would pray as many as a hundred times and almost the same during the night, even when I was staying in the woods and on a mountain. I used to rise before the dawn to say prayers through the snow, the ice and the rain and I thought no evil, nor was there any laziness in me – as now I see – because the spirit was fervent within me.

17. When I was there one night, during my sleep, I heard a voice say to me: 'You have done well in fasting – soon you will go back to your homeland'. And again, a short time later I heard a reply, saying: 'Look, your ship is ready'. It was not close by, but would

be about two hundred miles away and in a place I had never been before, where I knew nobody. Shortly after that I took flight, and left the man with whom I had been for six years, and travelled in the goodness of God who directed my way forward and I was afraid of nothing until I reached that ship.

18. On the day I arrived the ship was about to set sail and I said to them I was able to pay for my passage. But the captain was annoyed at my request and answered harshly and with indignation: 'There's no way you are going to travel with us'. When I heard these words I began to move away from them towards the place where I was staying, and as I left I began to pray, and before I could even finish praying I heard one of them shouting after me in a loud voice: 'Come quickly, the men are calling for you'. I hurried back to them and they said: 'Come, we will receive you in good faith, make friends with us in whatever way you wish'. On that day I refused to suck their nipples out of respect for God, hoping

they might come to faith in Jesus Christ, because they were gentiles. So I got my way in the end, and we immediately set sail.

19. After the third day we reached land and for twenty eight days we journeyed through a deserted region and they ran short of food and hunger overcame them.

The next day the captain began to talk to me, saying: 'Explain this, Christian. You say that your God is great and has power over everything, what's stopping you from praying for us? We are in danger of starvation and might not live to see another human being'. So I responded to them with confidence, saying: 'Turn with faith and with all your heart to the Lord my God, because with Him nothing is impossible, so that today he may send enough food your way for you to be satisfied, since all things with God are in abundance'. And with the help of God, it came to pass. Suddenly a herd of wild pigs appeared on the road right in front of our eyes, and they slaughtered many of them.

They spent two nights there gaining refreshment and the dogs were well fed too, though many had perished and been left along the road. After this, they gave great thanks to God and I was esteemed in their eyes and from this day forward they had food in abundance; they also found wild honey and offered some to me and one of them said: 'It is a sacrificial offering'. Thank God, I tasted none of it.

20. That same night, while I was sleeping, Satan assailed me violently, which I will remember as long as I am in this body. He came down upon me like a huge rock, so that none of my limbs could move. From wherever it arose in me – I don't know where – it came into my spirit that I should invoke the sun, and then I saw the sun rise in the sky and while I was crying out *'Helia!', 'Helia!'* with all my strength, the splendour of the sun fell upon me suddenly and immediately freed me from all the weight of oppression.

I believe I had been helped by Christ my Lord and that His spirit already then called out for me, as I hope it will be on the day of my deliverance, as the Gospel says: 'On that day' the Lord proclaims, 'it will not be you who speak but the Spirit of your Father which speaks in you'.

21. Once again, in addition to the many years that went before, I was held captive. On the first night I was with them, I heard an answer from a divine voice, saying to me: 'You shall be with them two months'. And that's exactly what happened. On the sixtieth night the Lord released me from their hands.

22. Along the way, the Lord provided food and fire and dry weather for us until on the tenth day, we crossed paths with others. As I have indicated above, we journeyed for twenty eight days through a land laid waste and moreover we had no food left on that night when we encountered others.

23. After a few years (then) I was back in Brittany with my relatives, who received me as if I was their son and begged me to

faithfully promise that after suffering so many hardships, I should never leave them again. And there I clearly saw in a vision of the night a man coming as it were from Ireland whose name was Victor, with countless letters. And he gave me one of them, and I read the beginning of the letter where it was written: '*The Voice of the Irish*'. And as I recited this first part of the letter, I thought in that moment I was hearing the voice of those near the Wood of Foclut which is close beside the Western Sea and then they cried out to me as if from one mouth, saying: 'We beg you, O Holy youth, to come and walk once more amongst us'. I felt heart broken and could read no further. And I woke up suddenly.

Thanks to God after so many years, their cries have been heard by the Lord.

24. And another night, whether it came from within me or beside me I do not know, God knows, through profound words I heard but could not understand except at the end of this oration when it was said:

'He is the one who gave his soul for you, He it is that speaks within you'. This time I woke up full of joy.

25. And again I observed that there was someone praying within me, as though I was inside my body and I heard beyond me, that is, beyond my inward self, that He was praying in sighs with great fortitude. During this I was left astonished wondering and thinking who it could be that was praying in me, but at the end of the prayer , He said it was the Spirit.

At this I woke up, and I remembered the Apostle saying: 'The Spirit helps the weakness of our prayers'. For we do not know how to pray as we ought to, but the Spirit Himself asks for us on our behalf with an ineffable groaning that cannot be described in words. And so again the Lord our advocate intercedes on our behalf.

26. And when I was put on trial by some of my seniors who came forward against my difficult ministry because of my sins, it's

true that on that day I was hit so hard I could have fallen here and forever. But the Lord spared his proselyte and stranger generously for his name's sake and he boldly came to my assistance in this trampling, as a result of which I did not fall apart badly even though shame and blame fell upon me. I pray to God there may not come a time when it is counted against them as a sin.

27. After thirty years they found a reason for going against me, something I had confessed before I was a deacon. Because I was feeling full of anxiety, with a troubled spirit I confided to my closest friend some of the things that I had done one day when I was young; it could have been in one hour because I had not learned how to control myself. I don't know – God knows – if I was fifteen years old then, and did not believe in the living God, as I had not done from childhood. I remained in death and unbelief until I was strongly chastised and humiliated by hunger and nakedness every day.

28. On the contrary, I did not willingly go to Ireland until I was almost weakened to death, but this was rather for my good because in consequence I had been corrected by the Lord, who trained me to be someone today who otherwise I could never have been, one who cares and labours for the well being of others, because at that time I did not care even about myself.

29. So this is what happened on the day I was rejected by the people mentioned above. As darkness fell, I saw in a vision of the night something written against my face that was defamatory, but at the same time I heard the voice of God saying to me: 'We have seen with displeasure the face of the designated one stripped of his name'. He did not say 'you have seen with displeasure', but 'we have seen with displeasure' as if He was identifying Himself with me, just as He has said: 'He who touches you (is) as the one who touches the pupil of my eye'.

30. Therefore I give thanks to Him who comforted me in everything, so as not to impede the journey on which I had

decided, to fulfill the work I had been encouraged to undertake by Christ my Lord. I know the virtue that increased in me derived from Him, and my faith gained favour before God and man.

31. This is why I can boldly say, my conscience does not trouble me now and will not in the future. God is my witness that I have not lied in the report I have given you.

32. But I grieve a lot more for my closest friend that we had to listen to the way he replied. I had confided my whole soul to him. And I was told by some brothers before that tribunal, at which I was not present, neither was I in Brittany – nor was it suggested by me – that he would fight on my behalf. He had even said to me from his own mouth: 'Look you should be raised to the status of a bishop' of which I was not worthy. Why was it then, afterwards, he disgraced me in public, in the presence of all that had gathered there, the good and the bad, about a matter for which he had before, freely and gladly exonerated me, as had the Lord, who is greater than all?

33. Enough said. But yet I must not hide the gift of God which he has lavished upon me in the land of my captivity, because I had sought for him strenuously and found Him there, and He saved me from all injuries – so I believe – through his indwelling Spirit that has worked in me until this day. I am speaking boldly again. God knows, if someone else had said this to me I would have remained silent, for the love of Christ.

34. Because of this, I give ceaseless thanks to my God, who kept me faithful in the day of my temptation, so that today I can confidently offer Him sacrifice, my soul as a living holocaust to Christ my Lord, who sustained me through many difficult times.

And so I can say: 'Who am I, Lord, or what is my vocation, that you have clothed me with such divine power so that today among the nations I should constantly exalt and magnify your name wherever I am, not only when things are going well but also during times of difficulty, so that whatever happens to me, good or bad, I must accept it in a balanced way and always give thanks to God who taught me how to trust him without reservation. He is the One who has understood me in my foolishness, so that during these last days I should dare to undertake this work so holy and so wonderful, providing the opportunity to imitate in some way those who have been commissioned by God before, to practice the teachings of His Gospel for all nations before the end of the world. We have all seen it happen now, so it is accomplished. Behold, we are witnesses that the Gospel has been proclaimed to the limit of human habitation.

35. Now, it would be tedious to give a detailed account of all my labour at every step or even in part. Let me tell you briefly how the most Righteous God has often liberated me from slavery and the twelve dangers that threatened the life of my soul, not to mention many treacherous attacks which I cannot speak about, so as not to cause injury to my readers.

But I consider God to be the author because he knows about everything even before it happens and never hesitated to warn me in divine messages, even the poor orphan that I am.

36. How then did I grow in wisdom, which was not within me before? I did not know the days of the earth were numbered or who God was. From where did this gift come from, which is so great and such a healing gift, to recognize and love God even at the price of losing my country and my parents?

37. Many gifts were offered to me with weeping and tears. I offended the donors, much against the wishes of some of my elders; but under the guidance of God, I chose not to accept or compromise with them. It was not because of me but God whose presence was strong in me and resisted them all. I had come to the people of Ireland to preach the Gospel and had to suffer great insults from non-believers as well as the reproach heaped on me after

going abroad; I had to face many persecutions even imprisonment, because I decided to give up my privileged life for the benefit of others. If found worthy, I am ready to offer my life voluntarily and without hesitation for His name, and so I long to expend it even to death, if the Lord would allow me.

38. Because I am deeply in debt to God, who gave me such grace that many people through me could be reborn in God and afterwards reach perfection and that clerics had to be ordained everywhere for them, for a people coming to believe for the first time, raised up by the Lord from the ends of the earth, as He once promised through His prophets: 'Gentiles shall come from the ends of the earth to You and shall say: How false are the idols our fathers got for themselves, for now they have become useless'.

And again: 'I have circled this place on the map for you, to be a light of salvation for the Gentiles to the end of the earth'.

39. And there I wait in expectation for the promise of the One who surely never deceives, as it is promised in the Gospel: 'They shall come from the east and the west, and shall recline with Abraham and Isaac and Jacob', just as we believe the faithful will come from all over the world.

40. For that reason, therefore, we ought to fish well and conscientiously, in the way the Lord advises and teaches when he says: 'Follow me and I will make you to be fishers of men'. And again He says through the prophets: 'Look, I send many fishers and hunters and others', says God.

That's why it was essential to stretch out our nets far enough for a huge multitude and gathering to be captured for God, requiring clerics everywhere to baptize and encourage the people in their need and longing, as God says in the Gospel and exhorts through His teaching, when he says: 'Go now and teach all nations, baptizing them in the name of the Father and the Son and the Holy Spirit, teaching them to observe all that I have entrusted to you. Behold! I am with you always even to the End of Time'. And again He says: 'Proclaim the Gospel to the entire world. Whoever believes and is baptized will be saved; but whoever is found wanting in belief shall be condemned'.

And again: 'This Gospel of the kingdom shall be announced to the whole world as a testimony before all nations, and then the end shall come'. The Lord proclaims through the prophets time and again saying: 'It shall come to pass, that in those days', says the Lord, 'I will pour out of my Spirit upon all flesh and your sons and your daughters will prophesy; your young people will see visions and your older people will dream dreams. Indeed, on all my male and female servants I will pour out my Spirit and they will prophesy.' And in Hosea he says: 'Those who were not my people I will call my people' and those who have never found mercy shall find it in that place where it is written: 'You that are not my people, shall be called the sons of the living God.'

41. That's what has been happening these days in Ireland as those without knowledge of God until now except through idols and filthy practices have now become the Lord's people and are called sons of God and the sons and daughters of Irish chieftains are seen to be monks and virgins of Christ.

42. Also there was one blessed Scots woman of noble birth, very beautiful and fully mature, who I baptized. After a few days, she was brought back to us for a particular reason. She revealed to us that she had received a message from a messenger of God who had counselled her that she should become a virgin for Christ and draw nearer to God. Thanks to God, six days later she eagerly embraced that noble choice. All virgins do this because of God even though their fathers disagree, causing them to suffer persecution and wicked and unjust reproaches from their parents; yet still their number increases (we are not sure how many from our own nation have been reborn in this way) including widows and those who have refrained from marriage.

But the women held in slavery suffer most of all having constantly to endure threats, intimidation and fearful abuses but the Lord gives grace to many of his female servants for although they are forbidden they courageously follow the example they have been given.

43. As a result, even if I had wished to leave them and go to Brittany – how I yearned to return to my homeland and my family – not only that but also to proceed further into the Gauls to visit the brothers and see the faces of the saints of my Lord; God knows how much I longed for this opportunity but I was bound by the Spirit, and it would have counted against me if I had done this because I have been designated to be their defendant in the future and I am afraid of losing the work I have begun not just for myself but for Christ the Lord who appointed me to come here and be with them for the rest of my life. If it is God's will, may I be guarded from making the wrong decision and seen as a sinner.

44. This is what I felt I ought to do but as long as I am in this body of death I do not trust myself for there is a strong force which strives every day to subvert me from the faith and from the purity of true religion which I have committed myself to for the rest of my life with Christ my Lord; but the hostile flesh is constantly dragging me towards death, in other words, towards the forbidden pleasures of what self desires.

And I know that in some ways I have not lived a perfect life as other believers but I trust in my Lord and am not embarrassed in his presence because I do not lie. Since the time I came to know Him when I was young, the love and fear of God has grown in me and from then until now thank God, I have kept the faith.

45. Laugh and revile me if you want to, I shall not keep silent, nor will I conceal the signs and wonders that have been shown to me by the Lord many years before things came to pass, seeing that He knows everything before it happens in the ages of time.

46. That is why I ought to give continuous thanks and praise to God for putting up with my foolishness not just once but on many occasions, sparing his intense anger towards me, the one given to be a helper but who was slow in response to what I had been shown by the urging of the Spirit.

The Lord has shown mercy towards me on thousands and thousands of occasions because he saw that I was ready but I did not always know what to do in the circumstances. For many have been opposed to this mission and have talked among themselves even behind my back and said: 'Why does this man place himself in danger among enemies who have no knowledge of God'?

This was not through malice – as I am a witness – I understood that it was because they had a problem with the fact that I was from the countryside. I was slow to understand the grace that was working in me; now I can see the things I should have known before.

47. I have, therefore, now put my case with simplicity to my brothers and fellow slaves who have trusted in me because of what I have forewarned and proclaim to strengthen and confirm your faith. I wish that you also could strive after greater things and achieve more. This will be my glory, for a wise son is the glory of a father.

48. You know and God knows too, how I have conducted myself since I was among you in my youth, in true faith and sincerity of heart. Towards the gentiles also among whom I live, I have been faithful and trustworthy to them and always shall be. God knows I have not deceived any of them nor would I ever think of doing so, out of respect to God and His church, so as not to incite persecution against them and all of us and to ensure that the name of the Lord will not be blasphemed through me; because it is written: 'Woe to that person through whom the name of the Lord is blasphemed'.

Image of Saint Patrick in stained glass from Magheralin Parish Church, Craigavon, Co. Down. Photo by Gigliola Siragusa.

49. Even though I am not wise in all matters, yet I have tried to keep myself safe for members of the Christian fraternity and virgins of Christ and for the religious women who freely gave me small gifts, which they hurled across the altar from their ornaments. I used to return these to them and they felt offended when I did that. But I had to, so as to secure a more lasting success, by making sure I retained a sense of caution towards everything, so I could not be accused of a dishonest ministry, preventing those without belief from having even the slightest opportunity to defame or undermine my ministry of slavery.

50. Should I perhaps have expected to receive a little something in exchange, for having baptized so many thousands of people? Tell me about it and I will return it to you. When the Lord ordained clerics everywhere because of the example given by my frugality – having charged them no fee for my ministry – if I had asked any of them for as much as the price of my

shoe; speak against me and I will return it to you.

51. I have spent too much on your behalf for anyone to trap me and I came among you and journeyed everywhere for your sake in many dangerous situations even to the farthest regions beyond which nobody lives and nobody had come to baptize or ordain clerics or rally the people. As a gift from God, I took these initiatives freely and conscientiously for your salvation.

52. During this time I gave gifts to the kings in addition to the wages I paid their sons who travelled with me, which did not prevent me being seized none the less along with my companions. On that day they were anxious to kill me, but the time had not yet come. They stole everything we had brought with us and bound me in irons until the fourteenth day when God set me free from their power and whatever belonged to us was returned through God's intervention and the friendship of certain relatives that we had previously secured.

53. You know full well how much I paid to those who act as judges through all the regions I used to visit most often. I think in truth I distributed among them nothing less than the price of fifteen men, so that you might be happy with me and I would always be happy in God for you. I cannot change my ways nor would I be happy doing so. My way is to spend and much more needs to be spent. The power of the Lord is great enough at some time in the future to take all that I have, for the sake of your souls.

54. So behold, I invoke God as witness to my soul that I do not lie. I am not writing to you to invite an occasion for flattery or greed or because I expect to be given respect from any of you. Sufficient is the honor that is not yet perceived but is believed in the heart. Faithful is He that has promised. He never lies.

55. But I see that in this present age I have been exalted beyond measure by the Lord, even though I was not worthy that he

should provide this for me. At the same time I know with absolute certainty that poverty and deprivation are more suitable for me than riches and refinery.

For Christ the Lord also was poor for our sakes while I, the unfortunate wretch that I am, have no wealth now even though I could easily have imagined it. I do not judge myself over this because every day I expect assassination or to be deceived or returned to captivity or whatever else might happen; but I fear none of these things because of the promises of heaven. I have cast myself into the hands of Almighty God, who rules everywhere, as the prophet says, 'Cast your thought upon God and he will provide for you'.

56. So now I commend my soul to my most faithful God, for whom I act as an ambassador in my unworthiness, although he pays no notice to status and has chosen me for this office to be one of the least of His ministers.

57. This is how I can return my offering back to Him for everything that happened to me. But what can I say or promise to my Lord? Whatever I can offer in return is nothing compared to what He has given me. I have considered my heart and the throne of my affections in the context of all (that He has given) and there is nothing more that I want than to be ready to drink from His Chalice as He gave it also to the others who loved Him.

58. Wherefore may God never allow it to happen to me that I should ever become separated from his people which He has purchased in the remotest parts of the earth. I pray that God will give me perseverance and consider me worthy that I should render to Him a faithful witness to the end of my life for the sake of my God.

59. And if I have ever done anything good for my God whom I love, I beg Him that He should give me the opportunity to pour out my blood for His name in the company of

those converts and captives even though I should be denied a grave or that my body is wretchedly torn to pieces limb from limb to be eaten by dogs or wild beasts or the birds of the air.

I have no doubt that if this happens to me I will have gained my soul and my body because without doubt on that day we will rise again in the brightness of the sun, that is in the glory of Christ Jesus our Redeemer, as sons of the living God and co-heirs with Christ, and to be become conformed to His Image because from Him and through Him and in Him we are going to reign.

60. For that sun which we see rises every day because He orders it so, but its splendour shall not last or reign forever. All those who worship it shall come to a miserable suffering; not so we who believe in and worship the true sun, Christ, who shall never perish, nor the one who has done His will, but he will be forever just as Christ is forever, who reigns with God the Father

omnipotent and with the Holy Spirit before the beginning of time, both now and for ever and ever. Amen.

61. And so let me again summarise the words of my Confession. I testify in truth and in exaltation of heart before God and His holy angels that I never had any other reason apart from the Gospel and its promises, to return to the people from whom I previously managed to escape.

62. I pray therefore to those who believe and fear God, whoever may happen to read or come upon this letter which Patrick, a sinner without education indeed, has written in Ireland, that no one should ever say that it was through my ignorance that I have tried to show forth these small things according to God's will and pleasure. It would be much better to understand and believe the truth, that it was all a gift from God.

And this is my Confession before I die.

The interior stairs at Dumbarton Castle.
From an old print by Pernot, 1827.

PATRICK'S LETTER
TO KING COROTICUS

PATRICK'S LETTER TO KING COROTICUS

1. PATRICK, a sinner without education, declare myself to be a bishop constituted in Ireland, appointed by God to be what I am. And so I live among barbarian tribes, a proselyte in exile for the love of God. He is a witness to this. I did not want to speak so harshly and pour out such bitterness from my mouth, but I am compelled by the zeal of God, roused in me by the truth of Christ, in support for my loved ones and sons for whom I sacrificed my homeland and parents and offer my life to the moment of death. If God finds me worthy I have vowed to teach the Gentiles even though some despise me.

2. With my own hand I have written and composed these words to be made public and delivered to the soldiers of Coroticus. I do not say, to my fellow citizens or to the citizens of the holy Romans but to the citizens of a nation of demons because of their evil works. Hostile to the core, they

live in death, allies of the Scots and apostate Picts. Men wallowing in blood with the blood of innocent Christians on their hands, including a number of those I won for God and confirmed in Christ.

3. The day after those who were newly baptized, being dressed in white garments and anointed with holy oil, the fragrance of which was still on their foreheads, were butchered without mercy and slaughtered by the sword by those mentioned above, I sent a letter with one of the holy elders I instructed from infancy, accompanied by clerics, asking for the return of what they had stolen and the prisoners they had taken captive but they mocked these messengers.

4. So now I do not know what I should grieve for most, those who were slain or those taken captive or those who have been dragged by the devil to such depths of depravity. They will be slaves in hell beside him as an eternal punishment because whoever commits this kind of sin is already a slave to sin and offspring of Zabulon (the Devil).

5. Therefore let everyone who fears God take note. As from now they are anathema to me and Christ my God for whom I act as an ambassador. Parricides! Fratricides! Rapacious wolves devouring the people of God as their daily bread as it is spoken: 'The wicked, O Lord, have destroyed your law', which in these last days has been well planted in Ireland, a land growing with the blessing of God.

6. I am not a usurper. I am a participant with those He has called and designated to proclaim the Gospel during these times when there is no shortage of persecution, to the ends of the earth – even if the enemy channels his evil resentment through the tyranny of Coroticus, a person who has no respect for God or priests chosen by God – who have been given the highest, most sublime divine power that whatever they bind on earth will be bound also in heaven.

7. For this reason I implore those of you that are holy and humble in heart to know it

is not acceptable to allow yourself be compromised by such people or eat and drink with them or accept any offerings from them until through penance, with the shedding of tears, they make amends to God and set free the servants of God and women baptized in Christ, for whom He died and was crucified.

8. The One who is Most High refuses the gifts of the wicked. The one who makes a sacrificial offering from what has been taken from the poor is like someone who sacrifices a son in the presence of his father. Those riches, as it is written, that a person has gathered from injustice, will be vomited up from his belly. The angel of death drags him away; he will be mauled by the fury of dragons. The tongue of the viper will kill him and he will be consumed by an unquenchable fire.

Woe, therefore to those who gorge themselves on stolen property; what is the benefit to such a man of gaining the whole world if he loses his soul?

9. It would take a long time to go through every specific detail from the law which applies in relation to such greed. Avarice is a deadly sin. You must not covet goods that belong to your neighbour. You must not commit murder. Homicide is incompatible with being a Christian and the one who hates another person counts as a murderer. In the same way, the one who lacks love towards others lives in death. How much greater, then (is the fault) of the one who has stained his hands in the blood of the children of God who have recently been purchased for God at the ends of the earth through our humble exhortations?

10. Was it without God or according to the flesh that I came to Ireland? Who compelled me? I was bound by the spirit not to see any of my family. Can it be held against me that I have such deep, spiritual compassion towards the people who once took me captive and devastated the male and female servants of my father's house? I was born free according to the flesh, my father was a Decurion.

I sold my nobility for the sake of others and I am not ashamed about this and have no regrets. The result is that I am now a slave in Christ to a foreign nation for no other reason than the unspeakable glory of everlasting life in Christ Jesus our Lord.

11. And if my own family do not want to know me (it is because) a prophet has no honour in his own country. Perhaps we are not of the same stock and do not have one and the same God as Father, as you have heard it said: He that is not with me is against me and he who does not gather with me, scatters. Is it not the case that someone can destroy and another will build up? I am not trying to be forward. It was not through my own merits but through the solicitude God has placed in my heart, enabling me to become one of the hunters and fishers God said would appear in the last days.

12. There is so much antagonism against me. What can I do, Lord? I am utterly despised. Look, the sheep around me who belong to you are being torn apart and

desecrated by the gangsters mentioned above, under the hostile directions of Coroticus. Far from the love of God is that person who betrays Christians into the hands of the Scots and Picts. Ravening wolves have gorged on the flock of God, which in Ireland at least was growing very well under great care, to the extent it is impossible to keep track of the number of the sons and daughters of Irish kings who have become monks and virgins of Christ. The wrong which has been done to the innocent should be unacceptable and even down to the underworld of hell it should not be tolerated.

13. Which of the saints would not tremble at the thought of celebrating or enjoying hospitality with such people? They have filled their houses with the trophies of dead Christians. They live on what has been stolen. Such wretches do not understand that what they offer to their friends and families is deadly poison just as Eve did not know that it was death she gave to her husband.

So it is for all who do evil. As a result of their actions, they bring upon themselves the punishment of eternal death.

14. The custom among the Romans of Gaul who are Christians is to send suitable holy men to the Franks and other barbarian nations with thousands of gold pieces to redeem the baptized from captivity. You prefer to slay and sell them to foreigners who have no knowledge of God. You hand over the members of Christ's body to what is essentially a brothel. What hope do you have in God? Or those who flatter you with the words you most like to hear? Let God be the Judge. For it is written: 'Not only those who do evil but also those who condone it, have to be damned'.

15. I do not know how to speak about this or what more can be said concerning those who have been killed among the sons of God, whom the sword has touched to such extremes of violence. For it is written: 'Weep with those who weep'. And again:

'If one part of the body is in pain let the other members grieve with it'. It is for this reason, the church grieves and laments for its sons and daughters who have not yet been slain by the sword, but who have been abducted and carried away to distant lands where sin openly, grievously, shamelessly abounds; where those free born have been sold. And worst of all, Christians are kept as slaves in houses of the abominable, depraved and apostate Picts.

16. Therefore I am wailing from deep within my heart in sorrow and grief, O my beautiful and beloved brothers and sons whom I have brought to birth in Christ beyond number – but what can I do for you now? I am not able to come to the aid of god or man. The abomination of the wicked has prevailed against us. We have become estranged like foreigners. It seems they do not believe in one baptism, or that we have one and the same God who is a father to us all. In their eyes, it is a disgrace that we are Irish. As it is written: Is God not the same for us both? Why then

have you allowed your neighbour to be forsaken?

17. All I can do now is grieve for you, so I grieve, you who are beloved to me. At the same time, I rejoice in my heart. I have not laboured in vain and my journey to another country was not without purpose. However despicable and depraved is the crime that has taken place, thanks be to God you who have left the world as believers who were baptized, have gone to Paradise. I can already see you have begun your journey to the place where night, grief and death will no longer exist. But soon you will leap like young cattle released from their ropes and you will trance over the wicked and they shall turn to ashes under your feet.

18. Then you will reign with the apostles and prophets and martyrs. You shall take possession of everlasting kingdoms as (Christ) himself testifies and says: 'They shall come from the east and the west and sit down with Abraham and Isaac and Jacob in the kingdom of heaven'. Dogs and those who poison and murder shall be kept

outside the doors and those who have lied or sworn falsely under oath shall find their place in everlasting fire. It was not without reason that the apostle says: 'When the person who is just can scarcely be saved, what hope is there for the sinner and those who have transgressed the law in such ungodly ways?'

19. Where, then, will Coroticus with his entourage of criminals find themselves? Rebels against Christ, who have been seen to distribute young baptized women as trophies in a miserable, temporal kingdom which will disappear in a moment? Like clouds or smoke blown away by the wind, so shall the wicked who are deceitful perish in the presence of the Lord but the just shall feast greatly in constancy with Christ; they shall judge nations and triumph over wicked kings for ever and ever. Amen.

20. I testify in the sight of God and his angels that it shall be so as has been revealed to me despite my limitations. These words are not my own but God's and the apostles and

prophets, who never spoke lies and which I have placed before you in Latin: 'The one who believes shall be saved but whoever does not believe shall be condemned'. God has spoken.

21. I implore whoever is a servant of God to be prompt in delivering this letter and that on no account, should it be suppressed or kept hidden by anyone but read openly among all people and in the presence of Coroticus himself. If God inspires them at some stage to recover their sense of God so that even at this late hour they should repent of their unholy deeds – the killing of those who are part of God's community – and they set free the baptized women whom they have taken as captives – there is still a chance they may live for God and be made whole as they deserve to be, both here and for eternity.

Peace, Father, Son and Holy Spirit.

HISTORICAL
BACKGROUND

307	Constantine Chlorus is Emperor in Britain.
314–337	His son, Constantine the Great, becomes the Emperor of Rome.
323	Birth of St Martin.
336	St Athanasius is exiled in Gaul.
357	Publication of Athanasius' Life of Antony.
360	Martin (aged 37) with the help of St Hilary, founds a monastery at Ligugé.
380	Magnus Maximus invited to marry Helen (Ellen) daughter of Eudes (Eudav Hen) a king of the ancient Britons.
383	Maximus declared 'King' and Emperor by the Legions in Britain under his command. Rebellion of Maximus. British Legions cross to Gaul landing at Aleth (St Malo) and at the mouth of the Rhine, attacking on

383	two fronts. Maximus takes over the Imperial Palace at Trier as a centre for his Command and displaces two incumbent Emperors. Valentinian flees and Gratian is killed in Paris. Maximus becomes Emperor of the West, in a treaty with Theodosius, Emperor of the East and is recognized as King by Sulpitius Severus. Martin lobbies Maximus in support of the Priscillians.
383	Calpurnius and his family leave Strathclyde in northern Britain and follow Conan to Brittany as part of the settlement under the new Emperor.
384	Birth of St Patrick?
385	Queen Helen (Ellen) develops a close relationship with St Martin.
385	St Augustine converts to Christianity.
385	Conan made King of Bretagne, Duke of Armorican Tract?

388	Martin warns Maximus that Valentianian is plotting to kill him. Maximus allows Priscillian to be executed.
389	In Brittany, Conan marries St Patrick's sister, Darerca.
389	Maximus is killed, beheaded at the third milestone from Aquilae by the forces of Valentinian and Theodosius.
393	Paulinas of Nola and his wife take vows of chastity and asceticism. Conversion of Sulpitius Severus to asceticism.
394	Severus visits Martin (aged 70) in his monastery on the Loire.
395	St Augustine writes the 'Confessions'. Severus writes 'Life of Martin' but delays publication through fear of retribution.
397	Death of St Martin: 11 November.

398-403 Irish King Niall of the Nine
Hostages raids Brittany.

400   Irish pirates attack the
Calpurnius estate near Bannavem
Tiburniae, in Brittany. Patrick, 16
years of age, is taken captive and
sold into slavery in Ireland.

405   Pelagius travels to Rome and
North Africa to challenge St
Augustine's doctrine of
'Original Sin'.

405   Threats of a Barbarian Invasion.
Roman troops leave Britain, to
defend Rome.

406   Dec. 31st. River Rhine freezes
again at Mainz. Barbarians cross
in vast numbers and rampage
through Gaul. Thousands killed.
Parts of Gaul become a
'wasteland'.

407   Patrick escapes from Ireland,
returns by ship to Brittany. He
returns home to his closest
surviving relatives then joins St

407	Martin's community at Tours for four years.
410	August 29th. Alaric enters the Salesian Gates, in the 'eternal city'. Rome falls to the Barbarians.
411	Patrick leaves St Martin's monastery on the Loire. Joins a community of 'barefoot hermits' in the 'Isles of the Tyrrhene Sea' located off the northeast coast of Brittany. Undertakes spiritual formation there for nine years, followed by seven years on another of these islands.
420	Augustine and Jerome write and campaign strongly against the 'heresies' of Pelagius and Priscillian.
421	Death of Conan in Brittany? Pelagius condemned, disappears, possibly killed.
421	Patrick 'sells his nobility'. Commissioned by St Senior on Mont St Michel. Patrick returns to Ireland as an Apostle?

423	Darerca (Conan's widow) goes to Ireland to help her brother Patrick in his Mission. Grallon appointed King in Brittany after the death of his father, Conan.
423	Grallon marries St Patrick's sister, Tigris (D'Agris).
429	St Germanus sent by Pope Celestine to Britain to combat 'the Pelagian Heresy'.
431	Palladius sent to Ireland by Pope Celestine as 'the first bishop to the Irish believing in Christ' (Prosper).
432	Traditional date given for St Patrick's return to Ireland as an Apostle.
459?	Patrick writes his Letter to Coroticus.
460?	Patrick writes his Confession. The Anglo Saxons take over Britain with greater force and genocide forces the ancient

460	Britons to migrate in large numbers from Wales and Cornwall to Brittany.
461	Traditional date given for Saint Patrick's death. Patrick disappears from all known historical and ecclesiastical records for the next two hundred years until ...
664	The Synod of Whitby. Wilfred acts as spokesperson for Rome. The Kingdom of Northumbria accepts the authority of the Roman Church, regarding tonsure and the Easter cycle.
672	Wilfred arranges for Dagobert II to marry Gizeles, Comptes de Razes. With Wilfred's support, Dagobert II is restored to the Merovingian throne in Gaul.
678	Dagobert II's assassination. Wilfred is implicated in this murder. His god-daughter marries Dagobert's widow, Gizeles de Razes (according to Lobineau).

679	Civil war in Ireland between 'Romani' and 'Hibernensi' – those who support Roman Reforms and those who hold allegiance to older Irish monastic foundations.
679?	'The Donation of Constantine', later proved a forgery, is published in Rome. Muirchú commissioned by the Church in Armagh to write a 'biography' of Saint Patrick.
680	The Anglo Saxons take the Kingdom of Strathclyde and pose a real military threat to Ireland.
682?	Tirechan writes a 'biography' of St Patrick.
697	Synod of Birr in Ireland. Adamnan, Abbot of Iona and a close relative of St Columba, actively seeks reform in the Irish Church. Roman reforms accepted.
697	St Patrick is accepted as Patron Saint of All Ireland, founder of

697	the Church in Armagh and is now officially recognised as Ireland's Apostle.
720	King Nechtan of the Picts evicts Irish monks. He declares his kingdom to be conformed with Rome.
780	The Welsh Church conforms to Rome.
795	Vikings attack Ireland and Scotland.
800	Charlemagne is crowned in Rome as the new Emperor.
1066	Battle of Hastings, the Normans takeover Britain.
1156	Norman Invasion of Ireland. The 'Romanisation' of Western Christendom is secured until the Reformation.